# CREATIVITY AND PROBLEM SOLVING

BRIAN TRACY

HarperCollins Leadership

An Imprint of HarperCollins

*Creativity and Problem Solving*



Published by HarperCollins Leadership, an imprint of HarperCollins Focus LLC.



Bulk discounts available. For details visit:
www.harpercollinsleadership.com/bulkquotes
Email: customercare@harpercollins.com

ISBN 978-1-4002-2213-1 (TP)

# CONTENTS

# Introduction

**CREATIVE** thinking skills are vital to your success. The average manager spends 50 percent or more of his or her time solving problems, either alone or with others. Your ability to deal with difficulties and solve problems will, more than anything else, determine everything that happens to you in your career. In fact, it is safe to say that an individual with poor creative thinking skills will be relegated to working for those with better-developed creative thinking skills.

The good news is that creativity is a *skill*, like riding a bicycle or operating a computer, that can be learned and developed with practice. In addition, there seems to be a direct relationship between the *quantity* of new ideas that you generate in your work and the level of success that you achieve. One new idea or insight can be sufficient to change the direction of a career or an entire company. The profitability, income, and future prospects of you and your company can depend on your creative contribution.

Remember, everything that you are or ever will be will come as the result of the way you use your mind. If you improve the quality of your thinking, you will improve the quality of your life.

This book is designed to give you a series of proven, practical methods and techniques that you can use, starting immediately, to generate a stream of life- and work-enhancing ideas. Every method in this book, when practiced, will give you better results than you are getting today. Sometimes the results will amaze you.

Unfortunately, the great majority of people do little or no creative thinking at all. They are stuck in a *comfort zone* where they strive to remain consistent with what they have done and said in the past. This is why Emerson wrote, "A foolish consistency is the hobgoblin of little minds."

They are missing one of the great opportunities for advancement and success that exists, and that is available to everyone.

Let's begin a whole new way of looking at the world.

# ONE

# The Root Sources of Creativity

**EVERYONE IS** creative. Creativity is a natural, spontaneous characteristic of positive individuals with high self-esteem. Companies that create a positive working environment receive a steady flow of ideas from everyone on the staff.

What are the factors that largely determine your creativity? There are three. The first is your *past experiences*. What has happened to you in the past has a major effect on determining how creative you are in the present.

## Influence of the Past

It seems that creative people, because of their backgrounds, consider themselves to be highly creative. Generating ideas is normal and natural for them.

Uncreative people, on the other hand, have often had negative environments, starting in childhood and continuing through different jobs, where they have generally accepted that they are not particularly creative at all. Even when they have good ideas, which they often do, they will reject or ignore the ideas, believing that if they are the source, the ideas can't be any good.

When you work (or have worked) for a company where your ideas are encouraged and stimulated, where your bosses and coworkers treat your ideas with respect and interest, you will feel yourself to be more creative in your job.

## Power of the Present

The second factor that determines your creativity is your *current situation.* Is there a lot of encouragement for new ideas in your workplace? Do people laugh together and get involved in discussing ideas together, or are your ideas ridiculed and criticized?

In the 1990s, Eastman Kodak was a $60 billion company with 140,000 employees. It dominated the world of film, as it had for many decades. Then, after many years of work, the scientists and researchers at Eastman Kodak discovered a new process called "digital photography" that did not require the medium of film to take and print photographs. When they took this discovery to their senior managers, they were roundly criticized and told, "This idea is no good; Kodak is a film company and this technology does not require film."

They were sent back to their offices and laboratories and told to forget about this new breakthrough technology. The rest is history. Within a few years, the Japanese camera manufacturers leaped all over the idea of digital photography, bringing out new digital cameras one after another, and soon, Kodak was finished.

## The Person You See

The third factor that determines your creativity is your *self-image*. Do you consider yourself to be a creative person? Do you see yourself as being highly creative, or not? Many studies indicate that 95 percent of people demonstrate the potential to perform at high levels of creativity. The work done by Howard Gardner at Harvard University concluded that there are several different ways of thinking, and that each person is a potential genius in at least one area. What this means is that the key to unlocking your creativity is to begin to think of yourself as a highly creative person.

## The Inner Game

Timothy Gallwey, in his book *The Inner Game of Golf*, teaches that the way to become a better golfer is to imagine that you are already a top golfer and to play golf as if you were already at championship levels. The very act of thinking about yourself as an excellent golfer improves your golf swing and your drive and putting almost immediately.

By the same token, the way to increase your creativity is to imagine that you are already a highly creative person.

Repeat to yourself, over and over, "I'm a genius! I'm a genius! I'm a genius!"

Visualize and imagine yourself as a highly creative person. Imagine that you are so creative that there is no problem in your world that you cannot solve by using your creative mind. Imagine that there is no goal that you cannot achieve by developing ideas for its accomplishment. Imagine that there is no obstacle that you cannot overcome when you apply your creative mind, like a laser beam cutting through steel, to remove the obstacle.

The good news is that everybody is inherently creative. Creativity is a tool provided by nature to man to ensure survival, and to deal with the inevitable problems and challenges of daily life. The only difference is that some people use a lot of their inborn creativity, and some people use very little.

***ACTION EXERCISES***

1. Identify your biggest single goal in life today. What is it, and what one action could you take immediately to move a step closer to that goal?

2. Identify the biggest problem or obstacle standing between you and your most important goal. What one action could you take immediately to solve that problem or remove that obstacle?

TWO

# Three Triggers to Creativity

**SOMETIMES PEOPLE** tell me that they do not feel they are particularly creative. I assure them that they are born with vastly more creativity than they could ever use. Their job is to stir up and unlock their inherent creativity.

I like to use this illustration: Imagine that you have poured yourself a cup of coffee and put sugar in it. You then put the cup to your lips, but the coffee still tastes plain and unsweetened. What has happened? The obvious answer is that you forgot to stir the coffee in the cup and mix the sugar throughout the drink.

Your creativity is very much the same. It is like the sugar at the bottom of the cup of coffee. It needs to be stirred up so that it dissolves and spreads through the entire cup of coffee.

## The Three Factors

Like stirring the sugar in the coffee, your creativity is naturally stirred up by three factors, all of which are under your control.

### INTENSELY DESIRED GOALS

The greater clarity you have about what it is you really want and the more positive and excited you are about achieving that goal, the more creative you will be, and the more ideas you will come up with. The more you want something, the more likely it is you'll find creative ways to accomplish it. This is why it is said that "there are no noncreative people, just those without goals that they want badly enough."

Determine the one goal that, if you achieved it, would have the greatest positive impact on your life. Write it down clearly on paper so that a child could understand your goal. This very action of deciding what you want more than anything else will almost instantly trigger ideas for actions that you could take to achieve that goal.

### PRESSING PROBLEMS

These are some of the greatest stimulants of all leading to greater creativity. If there is a problem or an obstacle that is stopping you from achieving something that is important to you, you will be amazed at how creative you can become in your ability to remove it.

Clarity is essential to creative thinking. Here is a way of gaining greater clarity: First, decide on your goal or objective. What is it that you really want in a particular area of your life? Then ask, "Why aren't I *already* at this goal or objective? Why haven't I *already* achieved this goal?"

Then ask, "Of all the reasons why I have not yet achieved my goal, what is the biggest and most important reason?"

Once you have identified the biggest single obstacle or difficulty that is holding you back from achieving your most important goal, your mind will start generating idea after idea to solve that problem or remove that obstacle.

### FOCUSED QUESTIONS

Your ability to ask yourself, and others, questions that force you to think deeply about your situation is a major stimulus to creativity. In his book *Good to Great*, Jim Collins says that a mark of great companies is that the executives are willing to ask themselves the "brutal questions" that force them to think deeply about their situation.

Peter Drucker is famous for saying, "I am not a consultant. I am an *insultant*. I do not give answers; I merely ask people the hard questions they need to consider to find their own answers."

Throughout this book, you will learn a series of questions that you can ask and answer to unlock more of your creativity and allow you to penetrate to the core of a subject. The more precise and focused the questions you use, the more rapidly your creative reflexes operate to generate workable answers.

## Test Your Assumptions

One of the most powerful ways to trigger creativity is for you to test your assumptions continually. Be sure that the goals, problems, and questions that you are generating are the real ones for your life and situation. It does you no good to focus on the wrong goals or on the wrong problems.

Continually ask yourself, "What are my assumptions?" Remember, many of your assumptions about your life, work, customers, money, the market, and other people are wrong or partially wrong. Sometimes they are completely wrong.

What are your *obvious* assumptions? What are your hidden or unconscious assumptions? And most of all, what if your most cherished assumptions were wrong?

False assumptions lie at the root of every failure. Whenever you are facing problems, resistance, or difficulties, ask yourself, "What are my assumptions? What if my assumptions are wrong?"

#### ***ACTION EXERCISES***

1. What one goal, if you achieved it, would have the greatest positive impact on your career or business?

2. What major assumption are you making in your business or personal life that, if it turned out not to be true, would require you to do something completely different?

THREE

# The Mindstorming Method

**DO YOU REMEMBER** the metaphor of stirring up the sugar in the coffee? You have enormous reserves of creativity that you can stir up and stimulate by using a variety of techniques. The Mindstorming method is one of them.

According to brain expert Tony Buzan, your brain has about 100 billion cells, each of which is connected directly and indirectly via ganglia and dendrites to approximately 20,000 other cells. Mathematically this means that the number of ideas or thoughts that you can generate is 100 billion to the 20,000th power, the equivalent of the number one followed by eight pages of zeros, line by line. The number of thoughts that you can think is greater than the number of molecules in the known universe. You are a potential genius!

## Pumping Mental Iron

Mindstorming is one of the most powerful ways ever discovered to creatively solve problems and achieve goals. It is a way of using focused questions for concentrating the power of your mind on a single question. In my experience, more people have become wealthy and successful using this simple method than any other type of creative thinking technique ever developed. In our seminars we call it "the 20 Idea Method."

The reason this method is so powerful is because it is so simple.

First, take a sheet of paper and write your most pressing problem or goal at the top of the page in the form of a *question*. For example, if your goal is to double your sales and profitability over the next two years, your question would be:

> What can we do to double our sales and profitability in the next twenty-four months?

The more specific the question, the better. An even better question is to define your goal numerically or financially.

> What can we do to increase our sales from $5 million per year to $10 million per year, over the next twenty-four months?

## Generate 20 Answers

You then begin writing answers, in the first person, using a specific action verb in your answer.

For example, you could say, "We hire and train twenty-two new salespeople." Or you could write, "We introduce three new products to our customers over the next twelve months."

You discipline yourself to continue writing until you generate at least 20 answers. You can do this on your own with a pad of paper, or with a group using a whiteboard or flipchart. But you must discipline yourself to generate a minimum of 20 answers in this exercise.

## Four Ways to Change

There are usually only four different ways that you can achieve any goal or solve any problem. First, you can do *more* of some things. Second, you can do *less* of other things. Third, you can *start* doing something completely new. And fourth, you can *stop* certain activities altogether.

As you generate your 20 answers, keep asking, "What should I do more of and less of? What should I start or stop doing?"

In this exercise, the first couple of answers will be fairly simple. You will easily conclude that you could do "more of or less of" certain activities.

The next five answers will be more difficult. You will be seeking things that you could start doing or stop doing.

The last ten answers will be the most difficult of all, and sometimes the 20th answer will be so difficult that you will feel like giving up. But you must force yourself to write at least 20 answers.

It is amazing how often we find that the 20th answer, the one that requires the hardest mental work to generate, is the breakthrough answer that transforms the business or changes a person's life completely.

## Aim for Quantity, Not Quality

Each time you generate and physically write down an answer, you loosen up and stimulate your creative abilities. Don't worry about quality, just quantity. Write down the first idea you think of, and then write down the opposite of that idea. Then write down a synthesis of the two ideas. Write down even ridiculous answers. Just force yourself to generate at least 20 answers, and surprisingly enough, sometimes an answer will jump off the page at you. Many of my students have found that this method helped them resolve a problem that they had been wrestling with for six months or longer.

## Take Action Immediately

Once you have generated 20 answers to your question, review them and select at least one idea that you are going to implement immediately. By implementing an idea immediately, you keep your creative juices flowing hour after hour. If you do this exercise first thing in the morning before you start off to work, you will find yourself thinking creatively all day long, just as if you had worked out physically in the morning. You will feel healthier and more alert all day.

One of the hardest things for anyone to do is something new or different. When you generate a great idea, you must immediately resolve to overcome the natural inertia that causes you to delay or procrastinate, the "comfort zone" that you can easily slip into, instead of taking action on the new idea.

You will have insights and ideas that will amaze you and the people around you.

***ACTION EXERCISES***

1. Take your biggest problem or goal today and write it down at the top of a page in the form of a question.
2. Discipline yourself to generate 20 ideas or answers to your question at one sitting, without getting up or moving around.

FOUR

# Questioning to Stimulate Creativity

**THE CREATIVE** mind is stimulated and triggered into action by focused questions. The more questions you ask, and the better they are, the more accurate and creative will be your thinking. Focused questions are the mark of a truly intelligent person. When you learn to ask focused questions of yourself, you can then ask focused questions of other people. Here are some of the more important questions.

## What Are We Trying to Do?

This is one of the most important questions to ask in business and personal life. It is amazing how many people are unclear about exactly what it is they are trying to accomplish at any given time.

Author Benjamin Tregoe once wrote, "The very worst use of time is to do very well what need not be done at all."

George Santayana wrote, "Fanaticism is redoubling your efforts when your aim has been forgotten."

Many people are working very hard in business, sometimes long hours and on weekends, but what they are working on is not particularly important or relevant to the overall goals and objectives of the business.

Whenever you feel that matters are moving too quickly, that you are achieving fewer and fewer results while working harder and harder, it is probably time for you to call a "time-out." Stop the clock. Close the door, turn off the electronic devices, and just ask the question, "What are we trying to do, really?"

*The Economist* magazine reported on a twenty-year study embracing 22,000 companies over ten years and using 150 researchers. The aim was to determine the level of managerial competence in a company and in a country, and the reasons for it. The researchers settled on three elements to determine overall managerial effectiveness: 1) setting clear objectives; 2) setting measures of performance; and 3) rewarding superior performance.

In every case, the ability to set clear objectives for the company, for each department or division, and for each person in the organization was the starting point of effective management that led to superior performance and results. What are you really trying to do?

## How Are We Trying to Do It?

Whenever you face problems, obstacles, resistance, or external challenges in achieving your personal and business goals, stop the clock once more. Think on paper. Look at the processes that you are using to get from where you are to where you want to go.

Could it be that you are on the wrong path? Could it be that the way you are attempting to achieve your goals no longer works, and may be obsolete, and you need to engage in completely different activities?

Geoffrey Colvin, a writer for *Fortune* magazine, wrote an article about business model innovation. His conclusion was that most companies are working with obsolete business models. Even worse, if you are in an information-based business, selling intangibles of any kind, the chances are perhaps 90 percent that you are going about your business the wrong way.

When Apple announced the iPhone in 2006, both Nokia and BlackBerry dismissed it as "a toy, a temporary fad that would soon be forgotten." They assumed that their market dominance was unassailable.

A BlackBerry executive said arrogantly, with regard to the iPhone, "Nobody wants apps." Today, Apple offers 1.2 million different apps that allow iPhone users to perform almost any business or personal function they want and numerous functions they had never dreamed of. By 2013, BlackBerry and Nokia market shares had dropped 90 percent and the companies were largely finished, relegated to the history books of business as market leaders that failed to ask, "How are we trying to do it? How are we trying to maintain our market dominance in cell phones?"

In what parts of your business could you be blind, as Nokia and BlackBerry were blind, to fundamental shifts and changes in your market that are rendering parts of your business model obsolete?

## What Result or Outcome Do You Desire?

What would be the ideal result or solution for a particular problem or goal you have today?

Imagine that you have a magic wand. You could wave this wand over your current business and make it ideal in every respect. If your current business situation, in terms of products, services, people, profits, and results, were ideal in every way, how would it be different from today?

Gordon Moore and Andrew Grove built Intel into a world leader in microchip production and a multimillion-dollar business. But the Taiwanese, Japanese, and Koreans began producing microchips of equal or higher quality at vastly lower prices, flooding the U.S. market and kicking the chair out from under the sales of Intel products.

As they tell it, one day Gordon Moore and Andrew Grove were sitting in Grove's office. They asked themselves the question, "If the board of directors of Intel fired us both and brought in new management, what would the new management do differently from us?"

They immediately agreed that new management would get out of the commoditized chip manufacturing business and shift all of Intel's assets and resources into manufacturing microprocessors for the new generation of personal computers. So that's what they did. They then went on to transform Intel into one of the biggest and most profitable companies in the world. They had the courage and the vision to ask the questions: What are we trying to do? How are we trying to do it? What result or outcome do we really desire?

## Are There Other Ways to Achieve Our Goals or Desired Outcomes?

Could there be a better way? If we were not doing it this way, what other way would be better, faster, cheaper, and easier?

Remember, there is always a better way. There is always a more efficient method to achieve any goal. There is always a superior way to use your special talents and resources.

Imagine that you have hired a high-priced management consultant to come in to your company to evaluate your current activities and strategies. This consultant sits down and begins to ask you some uncomfortable questions.

He wants to know what you are doing and why you are doing it that way. He wants to know what other ways you have considered to achieve the same goals. He wants you to tell him exactly what your goals and objectives are for your company overall, and for each part of your company that is expected to help you to achieve those goals and objectives.

Become your own management consultant. Imagine that you have hired yourself to come in and look at your business coldly, unemotionally, and with tremendous clarity. Ask yourself the "brutal questions."

***ACTION EXERCISES***

1. In twelve to twenty-five words, clearly explain exactly what you are trying to do in your business.

2. In twelve to twenty-five words, explain your plan of action to achieve your goals. How exactly are you trying to do it?

FIVE

# Brainstorming

## Unlocking the Power of Your Team

**BRAINSTORMING** is one of the most powerful techniques of all for developing synergy and unlocking creativity in a group, team, or organization. One of the chief responsibilities of effective managers is to conduct regular brainstorming sessions with their staff focused on business improvements. You cannot afford to leave the creative potential of your people untapped. You have to create an environment that encourages them to contribute their best ideas to the success of your business.

### The Brainstorming Process

Here are six guidelines for practicing brainstorming to stimulate people's creativity:

1. The ideal size of a brainstorming group is four to seven people. Fewer than four people tends to diminish the number and quality of ideas generated. More than seven people becomes unwieldy, with some people not getting a chance to contribute their best thinking.

When I conduct brainstorming sessions with larger groups, I break them down into groups of four to seven people and have them work separately, sharing their ideas with the overall group at the end of the session.

2. The length of an ideal brainstorming session is fifteen to forty-five minutes. Thirty minutes is optimal. It is important that you announce the exact time of the brainstorming session and then cut it off at exactly the agreed time. There is something about generating ideas toward a time limit that increases the quality and quantity of ideas considerably.

3. A brainstorming session's goal is to generate the greatest number of ideas possible in the time allowed. There is a direct relationship between the quantity of ideas generated and the quality of the ideas. Sometimes, the last idea generated during the last minute of the brainstorming session is the breakthrough idea that transforms the future of the organization.

4. The brainstorming session must be completely positive. This means that there is no judgment and no evaluation of ideas as they are generated. Every idea is a good idea. Your goal is to encourage the greatest number of ideas, and you do so by praising and encouraging even the most ridiculous ideas.

It is not uncommon for one ridiculous idea to be combined with another ridiculous idea to create a third idea that is revolutionary. Make it fun. Make it silly. Make it humorous. Make sure that everyone has a good time. The more laughter that occurs during a brainstorming session, partially because of the silliness of the ideas, the better the quality of the ideas and the greater the quantity will be. Aim for as many ideas or solutions as you can generate, and don't worry about whether or not they are good.

**5.** Before starting the brainstorming session, agree upon who is going to be the *leader*. The leader has the specific responsibility of ensuring that each person gets a chance to contribute. The best way to accomplish this level of participation is for the leader to go around the table, person by person, requesting one idea from each participant before moving on. This is an amazingly effective process. It is very much like starting an outboard engine. Once you have gone around the table once, everybody starts to become excited and involved. People will be throwing out ideas from all sides, waving their hands and fighting for airtime.

The job of the leader is to ensure an orderly process, encouraging each person to share ideas and making sure that each other person has a chance to talk.

**6.** Each brainstorming session also requires a *recorder*. This is the person whose job, along with contributing, is to write down the ideas as they are generated. In a particularly energetic brainstorming session, you may have to have more than one recorder because you will be generating so many good ideas. Whenever I conducted group brainstorming sessions with IBM, and with other companies, I would suggest having a competition between and among the tables about which group could come up with the most ideas. This idea of a "competition" caused everyone to put an emphasis on generating the highest quantity of ideas without judgment or evaluation.

## Nominal Group Technique

This is a simple but powerful technique that is used in brainstorming (as well as Mindstorming) to elicit creative answers to specific questions or problems. The simplest example of nominal group technique is *sentence completion exercises.* For example, you could complete the following three sentences with as many different answers as possible:

1. We could double our sales in the next ninety days if. . .
2. We could cut our costs by 20 percent in shipping and handling if. . .
3. We could become the leading suppliers of our product in this marketplace if. . .

Go around the table and complete these sentences, or other sentences that you make up, with as many different answers as possible. Assume that a logical, workable, and affordable solution already exists and is just waiting to be found. Your job is to provide the stimulus in the form of these sentence completion exercises, to elicit the very best ideas possible from the people involved.

Regular practice of this method will greatly increase the quality and quantity of creative thinking of everyone in your organization. This is an excellent way to find solutions that are right under your feet, but you are just not aware of them yet.

#### *ACTION EXERCISES*

1. Select one problem or goal that could make a major difference if it was solved or achieved in your business.
2. Assemble your brainstorming team, explain to them the process (described in this chapter), and then have them brainstorm as many ideas as possible to solve your problem or achieve your goal. You will be amazed at the result.

SIX

# Optimism Is the Key

**IN A 2013** study of the presidents of the 500 fastest-growing small companies, reported on in *Inc. Magazine*, the researchers discovered that the predominant quality of the executives was an incredible level of optimism regarding their companies, their products and services, and the futures of their enterprises. This optimism was not only infectious, permeating throughout their organizations and creating high levels of energy and imagination among the staff, but it also seemed to generate a continuous stream of ideas to help their companies become more successful.

An attitude of optimism can be developed and maintained in two different ways:

**1.** Think and talk about what you want and how to get it most of the time. Optimistic people think about their goals morning, noon, and night. They look at their world as being full of opportunities and are always asking *how* to achieve any goal or solve any problem.

2. Look for the good in every person or situation. Optimists are convinced that within every problem there is a solution. They believe that if they have a clear goal, they can also find a way to achieve that goal. When things go wrong, as they always will, optimists look for something good or beneficial that they can gain from each negative situation.

## The Language of Optimists

A characteristic of optimists is that they never use the word *problem*. Instead they neutralize that negative word by simply calling a reversal or a difficulty a "situation." They say, "We have an interesting situation facing us today."

Whereas a "problem" conjures up feelings of fear and loss, the word *situation* is neutral. You wrestle with a problem, but you simply deal with a situation.

An even better word is *challenge*. If a problem is something that you struggle with and that suggests setback and lost time or money, a challenge is something that you rise to, a situation that brings out the best in you and the people around you.

From now on, when something goes wrong, you can simply respond by saying, "We have an interesting challenge facing us today."

The best word of all is *opportunity*. When you begin to look into every problem or difficulty for the opportunity that it might contain, you will be absolutely astonished at how many opportunities you will see that you would have missed completely if you were bogged down in what initially appeared to be a problem.

One of the most important questions to ask when you have a problem of any kind is, "Why is this a problem?"

Because of the power of your superconscious mind, very often a reversal or a setback is sent to you as a "gift" to tell you that you are going in the wrong direction. Always look into any problem or difficulty as though it were an opportunity sent especially to you at this time to enable you to be more successful in the future. This way of thinking is the way of the superior executive.

## Seek the Valuable Lesson

You can remain optimistic in the face of any situation if you "seek the valuable lesson" in every reversal or setback. One of the great cosmic truths is that within every setback or difficulty, there are lessons that will help you to be even more successful in the future.

Here's an exercise: Identify your biggest single problem or difficulty today. Imagine that it has been sent to you as a gift, containing a lesson that you need to learn to move ahead more rapidly in that area of your life or business. What is the lesson?

## Feed Your Mind

To become a complete optimist, you need to "feed your mind" on a regular basis with positive ideas, information, knowledge, and conversations with positive people.

Just as you become what you think about most of the time, you become what you feed into your mind most of the time as well. If you eat healthy, nutritious foods, you will have a healthy and vital body. If you feed your mind with positive materials, you will have a positive and more intelligent and creative mind to work with.

When you develop this way of thinking in the face of every difficulty, you will be astonished at the excellent insights and lessons that you derive from every difficult situation in your life. Very often, the lesson you learn will be the key to your later success.

Positive thinking, positive speaking, and positive visualization—they are the catalysts that enable your superconscious mind to work at a faster and higher level than ever before.

Whatever you think about on a continuing basis you start to attract into your life. Like a magnet attracts iron filings, if you talk and think negatively, or if you worry about future events, you activate the Law of Attraction to bring those events into your life as well. Be careful.

Your superconscious mind requires clarity and commitment, conviction and *desire*. It is activated by intense emotion, the very best of which is desire. The more you intensely desire to be or have or do or achieve something important, the more rapidly your superconscious mind works to bring you insights and ideas that will help move you faster toward your goal, and move your goal faster toward you.

***ACTION EXERCISES***

1. Resolve today to become a complete optimist. Think and talk only about the things you want and how to get them. Look for the good in every situation. Seek the valuable lesson in every difficulty, and continually feed your mind with positive "mental protein," in the form of books, audios, DVDs, and conversations that are positive and life-enhancing.

2. Use the language of optimists. Avoid words that give negative connotations and replace them with words that energize and highlight solutions over problems.

SEVEN

# Develop the Qualities of Genius

**MANY MEN** and women throughout history who have been considered geniuses have been studied to determine their basic thinking processes, actions, and behaviors. Many of these people were found to have only average or slightly above average intelligence. They were not "geniuses" in the Einstein-like way.

However, they all seem to have three behaviors in common. Fortunately, these behaviors can be developed. As you practice these behaviors, you too can become more and more "intelligent." Master these three genius behaviors, and you'll become a genius at creative thinking and problem solving.

## Concentration

First, geniuses have developed the ability to concentrate single-mindedly, 100 percent, on one thing, to the exclusion of all distractions. This is sometimes called concentrated mind power (CMP), and it seems to accompany all great creative breakthroughs and accomplishments. Single-minded concentration, also called "single-handling," is essential to the achievement of important goals, the management of time, the completion of tasks, and all creative work.

Unfortunately, today most people are overwhelmed by an endless river of distractions, primarily technical. E-mail is constantly pinging with new messages, the smartphone is going off continually, the other phone is ringing, and messages are coming in nonstop. In addition, people in the workplace are continually interrupting and distracting each other. That's why people say, "You can't get any work done at work."

For you to learn to concentrate single-mindedly, you must create chunks of time, unbroken periods, where you can work without interruption or distraction.

Perhaps the most important time management principle, essential for creativity and concentration, is for you to "leave things off." Create zones of silence around you by disconnecting from all technology for specific periods of time each day. You require blocks of time (thirty, sixty, or ninety minutes) for your mind to settle down, like silt in a bucket of water. Only then can you get to the point where you can think with clarity and effectiveness.

## Seek Causal Relationships

The second quality of genius is the ability to see causal relationships, the big picture. Geniuses remain open-minded, flexible, and almost childlike in examining every possible way of approaching a problem.

Try looking at your work, yourself, and your business as part of an organic system. This means considering how every detail touches and influences everything around you. Instead of looking upon an event as a discrete and separate occasion, look at all the things that might have led up to the event, and all the things that may come after the event. Think of your situation as part of a bigger picture and consider all the different interrelationships.

Avoid *attachment*, or falling in love with a particular explanation or solution to a problem. One of the factors that puts the brakes on creative thinking is becoming attached or married to an idea that we've come up with. We then invest our ego in selling the idea to someone else. We consider ourselves successful if we can persuade someone else to come around to our point of view, even if there is a great possibility that our point of view is incorrect.

Like a Buddhist, try to stay detached from your idea and consider as many other ideas as possible with an open mind. Remain flexible, even with an idea that you think is incredible. Avoid the tendency to embrace the idea until you've looked at all the possibilities.

Treat your own idea as if it were suggested by someone else. Be skeptical. Ask questions. Begin with the assumption that the idea could be completely wrong.

## Use a Systematic Method

Third, geniuses use a systematic, ordered approach to solving each problem. They first define the problem clearly, in writing. Then they ask questions such as, How did this problem occur? Is this really a problem at all, or could it be an opportunity? Is this the real problem, or could it be indicative of an even bigger or different problem that needs to be solved?

In school, they teach you to think mathematically. Even though you never use algebra or geometry again after you leave school unless you enter a specialized field, the purpose of learning these subjects is to teach you to work systematically from the beginning to the end of a problem to find the solution. You learn a logical and systematic way to approach each problem, a skill that you can then apply in other areas of your life. All geniuses approach problems systematically, working their way through the problem step-by-step.

Remember, action is everything. You are what you do. When you practice the behaviors of geniuses, you very soon begin to perform at genius levels.

***ACTION EXERCISES***

1. Take a big problem that you are dealing with today and write down every detail about the problem on a sheet of paper. Sometimes, the answer will emerge as you write out the details.

2. Stand back from a problem you are wrestling with and observe the causal relationships between the problem

and other parts of your work. Take a sheet of paper, put a circle in the middle of the page with a definition of your problem, and draw branches, like spider legs, to circles on the periphery of the page with the names of different people and factors that are involved in this problem.

EIGHT

# Problem Solving in Seven Steps

**ANY ORGANIZED** method of problem solving is more effective in generating higher-quality solutions than no method at all. This chapter presents seven systematic steps for solving problems.

## Define Your Problem Clearly—in Writing

Writing is called a psychoneuromotor activity. By writing out your problem on paper, or on a whiteboard or flipchart, you are forced to use your *visual* sense, your *auditory* sense, and your *kinesthetic* sense. As a result, you activate your whole brain in the act of defining your problem clearly in the first place. Not surprisingly, fully 50 percent of problems can be solved by the very act of defining them clearly in advance.

In most cases where people have wrestled with a problem for a long time, it is because they haven't taken the time to clearly define the problem in the first place. Fuzzy thinking is a major obstacle to success in life and in the world of work.

## Read, Research, and Gather Information

Get the facts. McKinsey & Company is one of the most successful management consulting firms in the world. The "McKinsey Method" consists of, first of all, identifying the problem, and all variations of the problem, in advance. The second part is gathering information from every source possible, and validating every detail to make sure that it is correct rather than merely an assumption.

The more information you gather, the more likely it is that the correct solution to your problem will emerge from the data, like cream rising to the top of milk. Be prepared to follow wherever the facts may lead. Resist the temptation to fall in love with a solution early in the process and then to seek only that information that will confirm your initial conclusion. Keep an open mind.

## Don't Reinvent the Wheel

Remember that whatever problem you are dealing with has probably been solved by someone else, somewhere, and often at great expense. You don't have to reinvent the wheel. Ask questions of informed people and consult experts. Look for others who have had the same problem and find out how they dealt with it. You do not have to start from the beginning in most cases.

Perhaps the best time and money you can spend when solving a complex problem in your business is to hire a consultant or an expert in that field. By paying an expert a few hundred or a few thousand dollars, you can often save yourself a fortune in money and lost time. Some of the most costly mistakes I have made in business stemmed from my failure or reluctance to consult an expert before committing time and money to a business idea or project.

## Let Your Subconscious Work

Once you have assembled the information, and discussed it thoroughly with the other people involved, first try *consciously* to solve the problem. Think of everything that you could possibly do, and then, if you're not satisfied with the answers that you have generated, put it aside for a while. Set a schedule to revisit the discussion or problem at a later time when everyone has had a chance to think about it for a while.

In the Bible, it says, "Having done all, stand." What this means with regard to problem solving is that once you have been through the entire information-gathering process and you still do not have a solution, release the problem completely and get your mind busy elsewhere.

When you switch the focus of your attention from the problem or difficulty to something completely different that engrosses your mind completely, your *subconscious* and *superconscious* minds begin to work on the problem twenty-four hours a day, like a supercomputer processing a complex formula or series of numbers. By turning your problem over to your higher mental powers, and just relaxing and getting your mind busy elsewhere, very often this higher mind will bring you the answer you need, exactly when you require it.

### Use Your Sleep

Review your problem just before going to sleep, and ask your subconscious mind for a solution. This seems to work particularly well when you have a difficulty or a dilemma that you must deal with the following day. By requesting a solution, you will often wake up with a perfect answer or solution to the problem that you have to deal with that day. You may wake up in the middle of the night with an answer or an insight. You may wake up in the morning and the answer will be right there, just like a butterfly landing on your shoulder.

### Write It Down

It is a good policy always to have a notepad handy so that you can jot down these answers and ideas and insights at any moment, rather than forgetting them, as often happens. When you get that breakthrough illumination, be sure to write it down quickly. One good idea can often save you years of hard work. One good idea can be all you need to start a fortune.

### Take Action

Finally, whatever the idea, take action on it immediately. Don't hesitate. Very often, the ideas that come to you are "time dated." If you take action immediately, wonderful things can happen. But if you wait to take action for a few hours or a few days, you can often miss the moment. Don't let that happen to you.

***ACTION EXERCISES***

1. Take any problem or goal that you have and put it into "Google keywords." Download all the articles and blogs that have been written about your particular problem or goal and review them carefully. You may be astonished at what other people have already found and what other people are already doing.

2. When you are clear about your problem or goal, ask around and look for others who may have already solved this problem in their own lives or work. Ask others if they might know someone who might know something about the problem you are working on. You may be astonished at how quickly you find exactly the right person to speak to.

NINE

# Mind-Stimulating Exercises

YOU HAVE heard it said that knowledge is power.

But only practical knowledge—that is, knowledge that can be applied to some purpose to achieve a result or benefit—is truly powerful. If knowledge was everything, all librarians would be rich, because they are surrounded with millions of words of knowledge.

The exercises in this chapter will help you identify the goals and problems to which you want to apply your creativity and knowledge.

## The Quick List Method

The first exercise is to write, in thirty seconds or less, the answers to the following question: What are your three most important goals in life right now?

This is called the Quick List method. When you only have thirty seconds to write down your three most important goals in life, your real goals will pop out on the page, sometimes to your surprise.

When I give this exercise to my seminar attendees, more than 80 percent of the people in the audience will write down the same three goals: a financial goal, a family goal, and a health goal. This is as it should be. These areas turn out to be the three most important goals in the life of almost every person.

Once people have answered this question, I ask them to give themselves a grade of one to ten on how satisfied they are in each area. In whichever area they give themselves the lowest grade, that turns out to be the area of their lives where they are experiencing the most problems or unhappiness. Try it for yourself and see.

In our business seminars, we expand this exercise by asking business owners and executives to answer a series of Quick List questions that focus specifically on business, financial, sales, product, people, and competitive goals. Participants have thirty seconds to write down their answers to each of these questions. Their answers are quite revealing and often business-transforming.

## The Brutal Questions

Leadership is the ability to solve problems. Success is the ability to solve problems. The only thing that stands between you and achieving all your goals are problems and obstacles of some kind. What are they? The next exercise is to focus on what Jim Collins calls "the brutal questions"—those questions that force you to focus on your problems.

You can start with this general question: What are our three most pressing problems today? You can then expand this question to embrace every important area of your business. You can ask:

1. What are our three biggest business problems today?
2. What are our three biggest financial problems today?
3. What are our three biggest sales problems today?
4. What are our three biggest competitive or market problems today?
5. What are our three biggest people problems today?
6. What are our three biggest product or service problems today?
7. What are the three most important steps we can take immediately to improve our business results?

Your ability to ask and accurately answer these questions, and then to implement solutions to the problems that you identify, is a critical determining factor in the success of your business.

## Use the 80/20 Rule

The 80/20 rule seems to apply to both business and personal problems. In this case, it means that fully 80 percent of your problems, obstacles, difficulties, worries, and concerns are *within* yourself or your business. Only 20 percent are determined by *external* factors or people.

The starting point of the superior thinker is to identify the problem clearly and then ask, "What is it in me, or in my company, that is causing this problem?"

## Identify Your Favorite Excuses

In business seminars we always ask, "How many people here would like to double their profitability?"

Everyone in the room raises their hand. We then ask, "Why aren't your profits already twice as high as they are today?"

That's when I point out that there are lots of companies in the same industry that are earning two times, five times, and ten times as much as they are. Many of these companies with higher earnings have not been in business as long as the people in the room. All of these companies face the same competitive environment as the business owners and executives taking my seminar. Why is it that they are earning so much more money than you are?

This exercise helps people to identify their favorite excuses for less-than-ideal financial performance. Why isn't your business twice as big? What are your favorite excuses? What do you tell yourself, and others, to let yourself off the hook of higher performance?

What is it in you, or inside your company, that is holding you back?

Asking and answering these questions continually will stimulate your creativity, giving you ideas and insights that will allow you to solve any problem or overcome any obstacle that may be holding you back from achieving your business and personal goals.

## Practice Idealization

Leaders have vision. Vision is the ability to imagine an ideal future state, and then to come back to the present and develop a plan to get from where you are today to where you would like to be at some time in the future.

If you could wave a magic wand and make your future business perfect in every respect, what would it look like? How would it be different from today? And most important, what would be the first step that you would have to take to get from where you are to where you want to go?

Decide today the first step that you are going to take, and then act immediately. Everything else will flow from that. The good news is that you can always see at least one step ahead. You may not be able to see the entire path to your future, but you can always see one step. And if you go as far as you can see, you will see far enough to go even further.

Idealization is a proven method of "peak performance thinking." By projecting forward into the future and imagining a perfect state, and then by looking back to the present where you are today, you often gain a wonderful perspective and see all kinds of things that you can do, starting today, to begin to create that perfect business of the future.

## The Magic Question

Here's a fun exercise. Ask yourself: "What one great thing would you dare to attempt if you knew you could not fail?"

Imagine that you still have your magic wand. You could wave this magic wand and achieve any one goal in life. If this were possible for you, what one goal, if you achieved it, would have the greatest positive impact on your life?

Whatever your answer—and you always have an answer—write it down, make a plan, and begin to work on it every day. Take the first step. Do something. Do anything. But begin to work every day on this major goal, the one goal that can make all the difference in your life if you achieve it.

***ACTION EXERCISES***

1. Write down your three most important goals in life—business or personal. Write them down, right now.
2. Identify the one goal which, if you achieved it, would have the greatest positive impact on your life.

TEN

# Use Your Three Minds for Thinking

**EACH PERSON** has three different "minds" with which to think, solve problems, make decisions, and achieve goals. Your ability to understand the differences among these three different minds and to maximize their potential to improve your life and business can transform and multiply your results.

## The Conscious Mind

This is the awake, alert mind that you use whenever you are busy and active. The conscious mind is objective, analytical, rational, critical, and pragmatic. It takes in information from many sources, analyzes the information, compares the information with other information that has been stored in memory, and makes decisions. Your conscious mind is the place where new information enters your brain, like a doorway.

Daniel Kahneman, in his bestselling book *Thinking, Fast and Slow*, explains that you have two ways of using your conscious mind almost all the time.

The first way, "fast thinking," is intuitive, automatic, instinctive, and immediate. This is the thinking style in your conscious mind that you use to navigate the rapidly unfolding events in your daily life activities. Fast thinking is very much like driving through traffic; you are making quick decisions, reacting and responding to changing events, as you move along. Most of your time during the day is spent in fast thinking. You utilize fast thinking in conversations, telephone calls, and in your replies to e-mails and responses to external demands. This is the normal and natural use of fast thinking, and it is quite appropriate in most cases.

**THINK SLOWLY**

The second form of thinking described by Kahneman is "slow thinking," which is another function of your conscious mind. This type of thinking requires that you slow down the pace of thinking and give careful consideration to what is happening before you say anything or react in any way.

The proper use of slow thinking is when you are engaged in any activity or making any decision that has long-term ramifications or consequences. For example, strategic planning in a business forces all participants to engage in slow thinking.

This is absolutely essential because the decisions made in strategic planning have long-term consequences and can largely determine the success or the failure of the enterprise.

One of Kahneman's great insights is that people too often use fast thinking when slow thinking is required. Instead of taking a time-out and carefully considering all the facts and details of a major decision, many people use fast thinking and inadvertently make commitments and decisions that have long-term ramifications.

### THINK ON PAPER

One of the best ways to switch from fast thinking to slow thinking when it is more appropriate is by asking questions and thinking on paper. The very act of asking questions forces you to slow down and think much better about the issue at hand. Writing things down on paper, especially when you are assembling all the facts or details concerning a situation, forces you to think slowly.

The rule is that you will always make better decisions if you take more time to consider them in advance. Whenever possible, you should "buy time" when making an important decision of any kind. Delay the decision for twenty-four hours, a weekend, a week, or even a month if you possibly can. Without exception, the more time that you take to think slowly about an important decision, the better-quality decision you will make when you finally choose to act.

## Your Subconscious Mind

This is the great powerhouse or library part of your mind. It takes in and stores all experiences, knowledge, decisions, ideas, and thoughts that you have ever had. And it can access this memory almost instantaneously. Your subconscious mind records and recalls all data; it remembers everything and is capable of combining existing information into new forms and patterns to solve problems.

### TRUST YOUR INSTINCTS

Peter Ouspensky, the metaphysician, said that your subconscious mind functions 8,000 times faster than your conscious mind. An example is the intuitive response we have to new people. Throughout your life you will meet different people; some of them you will instantly like and some you will instantly dislike. This complete assessment usually takes place in less than four seconds. Later, you will find that you had good reasons for liking or disliking, trusting or not trusting another person. But at the instant of meeting, it was as if your conscious mind took a snapshot of the person's face, passed it on to your subconscious library, and instantly compared that face against every other facial experience that you have ever had to give you an instant feeling that was either positive or negative.

A major purpose of your subconscious mind is to make all your words and actions fit a pattern consistent with your self-concept, your basic belief system. Your subconscious mind controls your body language, your tone of voice, your levels of self-confidence, and your feelings of competence or ability in any situation.

### FILL YOUR MIND WITH POSITIVE THOUGHTS

When you feed your conscious mind a steady stream of positive ideas, messages, and pictures, this information is passed directly to your subconscious mind and begins immediately to affect the way you think and feel about yourself.

Earlier, I mentioned how important it is for you to repeat the words "I'm a genius!" over and over. When you first say these words, or almost any other positive words to yourself, you may feel a little uncomfortable. But as you repeat the words over and over again, you wear down the resistance in your subconscious mind to this new self-concept. Eventually, your subconscious mind accepts your new command as your new reality. It then goes to work to make sure that everything you do, think, say, and feel is consistent with the new pattern that you have programmed into your subconscious mind.

## The Superconscious Mind

This is the most powerful mind that you have. Almost all great accomplishments in human history have been accompanied by superconscious ideas and inspiration. Your ability to tap into and use your superconscious mind on a regular basis is your key to unlocking your creative genius in every part of your life.

The superconscious mind is sometimes called the *collective unconscious.* It is also called the *universal subconscious mind* or *infinite intelligence.* Carl Jung called it the "superconscious" and said that it was the source of all originality and creativity in the human universe.

The superconscious mind is the starting place of all creative breakthroughs, insights, intuition, inspiration, and imagination. This mind works continuously on a nonconscious level to solve problems, remove obstacles, and move you toward your goals.

When you clearly define, in writing, a goal that you want to achieve or a problem that you want to solve, this information is passed on automatically to your subconscious mind. Your subconscious mind then transfers it to the supercomputer of your superconscious mind, which then goes to work to help you achieve your goal or solve your problem twenty-four hours a day until the answer comes.

## Integrate Your Three Minds

Remember, you are a potential genius. You have 100 billion brain cells, each connected to as many as 20,000 other cells, giving you a thinking capacity beyond that of the biggest supercomputer that can ever be built.

You can use your mind for good or ill. By using your conscious mind to develop absolute clarity about what you want, and then by visualizing your goal and writing it down so that it is transferred to your subconscious mind, you use your thinking powers at a higher level. When you confidently and calmly expect and believe that your superconscious mind is working twenty-four hours a day to bring you exactly what you want at exactly the right time, you activate your superconscious powers and take complete control of your mind.

By using all three of your different minds in harmony, you unlock the genius that exists within you.

***ACTION EXERCISES***

1. Take the time to think slowly and develop absolute clarity about what you want and what it will look like when you achieve your goal. Write it down clearly so that a child could understand what you really want.
2. Repeat positive words over and over again. "I'm a genius" is one suggestion, but use whatever phrase you respond to best.

ELEVEN

# Practice Two Approaches to Thinking

**THE WAY YOU** think either inhibits or liberates your inborn creativity. Your particular thinking style is learned, starting in early childhood, usually as the result of imitating one or both parents. You learn how to think the way your parents think when you are too young to be aware of what is happening.

Different styles of thinking are usually survival or coping mechanisms. They are developed unconsciously and unthinkingly as a response to the uncertainties and unpredictability of the world around you. The good news is that because these thinking styles have been learned, they can be unlearned as well. You can, with continual practice, actually override or cancel out an unhelpful way of thinking with a positive and more dynamic way of thinking.

## Mechanical Thinking

If you take the various thinking styles and arrange them across a spectrum, you will have mechanical thinking at one extreme and adaptive thinking at the other.

Mechanical thinkers are rigid, inflexible, and quite fixed in their ideas and opinions. They rely on what is often described as "rote thinking" or automatic thinking; they are unbending in their ideas and interpretations of the world and are not open to any ideas or opinions that deviate from what they have already decided to think.

Mechanical thinking is also a form of "normative thinking," where the individual sees everything as one extreme or the other, black or white, wrong or right, with few distinctions in between.

### WHY IT WON'T WORK

Mechanical thinkers tend to be pessimistic and to look for reasons why anything new or different won't work or can't work. In NLP they call this "sorting by differences." This type of person continually seeks out how anything that you say or suggest is different from what has happened in the past or what the person currently believes. Once the person sees a difference or a conflict, your idea is immediately downgraded and discarded.

Mechanical thinking is noncreative. The favorite word of a mechanical thinker is the word *no.* These people have what is called psychosclerosis, or a "hardening of the attitudes."

How do you deal with mechanical thinkers? You put them into jobs or positions where no creative thinking is necessary. Most governments are staffed with these people from top to bottom, which is why it is so hard to get a government official to be open to a better or different way of doing something.

Mechanical thinkers make good accountants, engineers, and data programmers. They score high in the personality tests on "compliance" and "stability." They are most comfortable in situations that are totally predictable and where no variation or turbulence is to be expected. They are not particularly creative, and they are quite happy that way. In fact, mechanical thinkers are largely convinced that other people, those who are more flexible and open to new ideas, are less stable and less capable than they are.

## Adaptive Thinking

Adaptive thinking is characterized by a high degree of flexibility in approaching any project, problem, or goal. As we mentioned previously, this way of thinking is characteristic of geniuses and highly creative people. This is the kind of thinking that you want to practice on a regular basis.

As it happens, some people are mechanical in some areas of thinking and adaptive in others. Some people are very rigid with regard to their political or religious convictions, but very relaxed and casual with their opinions in other areas. The ideal is for you to become an adaptive thinker in as many areas as possible.

### KEEP YOUR MIND OPEN

Adaptive thinkers have an open mind. They avoid falling in love with their own ideas. They practice detachment and can stand back from an idea, as if someone else had come up with it and they had been asked to evaluate it objectively.

Adaptive thinkers are more flexible and willing to look at many different sides of a question. They are optimistic in that they believe that problems can be solved, and they are constantly looking for innovative or positive solutions to the most difficult challenges.

Adaptive thinkers are creative, imaginative, and ask many open-ended questions: Why? When? Where? How? Who? and Which?

The key to becoming an adaptive, highly creative thinker is for you to suspend judgment on as many things as possible, especially at the beginning. The very act of refraining from judging, and instead keeping an open mind, makes you naturally more flexible in your thinking.

Finally, if you do make a decision and you get new information that invalidates your decision, be willing to change your mind. Refuse to become locked into a particular idea or conviction, especially when the evidence is against you.

***ACTION EXERCISES***

1. Challenge your self-limiting beliefs about yourself, especially about your talents, abilities, and potential. What if none of them were true? What if you had unlimited potential and all you had to do was to learn how to release it?

2. Think of a situation that is causing you a good deal of frustration or anger today. Imagine that you are completely wrong in the position that you are taking, and the other person is completely right, or that there is a way of dealing with this situation effectively that is completely different from anything you have thought of up till now.

TWELVE

# Practice Lateral Thinking

**LATERAL THINKING** forces the mind out of comfortable or conventional ways of thinking. It was pioneered by Edward de Bono in England. One way to illustrate lateral thinking is to remember that when people find themselves in a hole, their natural tendency is to dig the hole deeper. However, the solution may be to go somewhere else and to dig a totally different hole.

Lateral thinking is used to break your pattern of habitual thinking, or the tendency to fall into the trap of the comfort zone and continuing to do things the same way you have always done them in the past.

## Reverse Keywords

One method of lateral thinking is the reversal of keywords or phrases. For example, as I mentioned previously, refer to a problem as an *opportunity*. With that in mind, treat the problem as though it has been sent to you as a gift. Examine it for the opportunity that it might contain.

Instead of saying "Our sales are down," say, "Purchases are down." It isn't that we are not selling enough, but our customers are not buying enough. This changes the whole focus of the situation and leads to completely different solutions from the original definition.

Another method of lateral thinking is to use *random association*. Here, you pick words and then force them to fit your situation. Take a word such as orange or artichoke and describe your business, product, or problem as that word.

For example, you could say, "Our business is like an orange because . . ." On the outside it looks pretty smooth, but as you get close you see a lot of bumps. Inside you find a lot of seeds and membranes and divisions of the orange into a series of separate departments that may not communicate with each other. Of course, there are some juicy parts of our business (the most profitable parts) that we may not be paying close enough attention to. The practice of random association often triggers creative thinking in a way that you had not expected.

## The Dominant Idea

Another approach in lateral thinking is called "the dominant idea." If the dominant idea is that we have a real problem here, the lateral thinking alternative should be that we have a real profit opportunity or cost-cutting opportunity.

Shift your thinking away from the dominant idea. For example, rather than saying "We need to sell more," say "Our customers need to buy more.

Maybe a failure you are experiencing or a loss that you are suffering is nature's way of telling you that you are on the wrong road. Perhaps you should be doing something different, with a different product or service, selling to a different market. Maybe a loss that you're suffering today will enable you to make a profit by doing or changing something else.

To practice lateral thinking, you should look at the other person's viewpoint and try to see and describe the situation through that person's eyes, especially your customers. Lawyers do this when preparing a case for court. They will first of all argue the case from the opponent's side before preparing their own case against the other party.

## Think About Customer Development

The greatest breakthroughs in sales and marketing today, described in *The Lean Startup* and *The Four Steps to the Epiphany*, revolve around the focus on "customer development" rather than "product development." This requires taking the time to thoroughly study the demographics, the psychographics, and then the ethnographics of your potential customers. Take the time to learn who they are and what they really want and need, and then develop your products and services based on that information.

## Fantasizing

Fantasizing is another way of practicing lateral thinking. Imagine that you had a magic wand and you could wave it to remove all obstacles to achieving your objectives. If that were to happen, if you waved this magic wand and all your problems or obstacles disappeared, what would your situation look like?

Pretend the obstacles are not even there. What difference would that make? What would you do differently? What new possibilities or opportunities would open up for you if you had no limitations in terms of time, money, people, resources, talents, or abilities? Then, figure out a way to achieve these goals even without removing those obstacles, and even without having all of the natural advantages you could desire.

### *ACTION EXERCISES*

1. In what way does your company compare with an orange, and how could you change your structure to become more productive and profitable?

2. What is it that your customers of tomorrow really want and need, and are willing to pay for, that is different from today? How could you bring those products and services to market?

THIRTEEN

# How Your Mind Works

**YOUR MIND** is a wondrous thing, an incredible processor of information that you take in through all your senses. As it happens, each person has a dominant thinking style, a specific way of processing information, taking it in, and using it in the best ways possible.

There are three basic types of information processing used in creative thinking:

**Visual**
Visual people think in terms of pictures, written words, images, charts, and graphs. They have to "see" the problem or information in order to understand it. They will say, "I see what you mean."

**Auditory**

Some people need to hear ideas, discussions, sounds, and music. They will say, "That sounds good to me," or "That doesn't sound right for me."

**Kinesthetic**

Kinesthetic people are more attuned to their feelings, emotions, movement, or touch. They have to get a "feeling" for the problem or situation. They like to pick things up, hold them, turn them over in their hands, and feel them. They like to move around rather than sit still during conversations. The will say, "That feels right to me."

## Try Them All

When you are working to solve a problem, you should try them all, especially with a group of people who may have different processing styles. Write things down. Talk about them and invite discussion. Stand up and walk around, and encourage others to move around, too.

Looking at pictures or drawing graphs and diagrams is a wonderful way for a visual thinker to get insights and to understand the problem or situation at greater depth.

Encouraging discussion, saying things out loud, and dialoguing about a problem or a situation is helpful for an auditory thinker.

To activate the kinesthetic senses, you should write things down, talk out loud, walk around and move. Sometimes, going for a walk in the park or just getting up and taking a break is an excellent way for a kinesthetic thinker to get breakthroughs in problem solving.

## Lessons from Giving Effective Seminars and Workshops

When I began giving seminars, quite without thinking about it, I would lecture, write things down on a flipchart or a whiteboard, encourage people to take notes, and then ask them to discuss what these new ideas meant to them. Inadvertently at first, I was activating the visual, auditory, and kinesthetic processing modes of everyone in my audiences.

Participants were always amazed that they would still be alert and highly energized, even after eight hours of this type of seminar or workshop. It was because their entire brains were fully activated throughout the day.

## Identify Your Predominant Style

Each person uses visual, auditory, and kinesthetic thinking—but we each have a predominant or favorite way that we think. Be sure to try all three, especially when you're working with a group of people on a problem or decision. Assume that people in the group will need to be appealed to in different ways. Sometimes you can give people pages of numbers and they won't even look at them because they are auditory or kinesthetic thinkers, and not visual.

## Give People Information the Way They Like It

Peter Drucker points out that one of the most important things you need to do is to find out how your manager prefers to process information. If your manager is a visual thinker, be sure that you write everything down in your reports so that you can discuss items, point for point, visually. If your manager is an auditory person, you can explain the situation verbally and your manager will absorb the information comfortably. If your manager is a kinesthetic thinker, he or she will probably want to touch or feel your materials and get up and physically move around during your discussions.

When you present a written report to an auditory processor, he will ask you, "Give me the bottom line; what does it say?" If you are dealing with a visual processor and you tell her news or information, she will probably ask, "Could you write that down for me?"

The more you can include all three forms of processing when you are solving problems or making decisions with your staff, the better and more insightful ideas and solutions you will come up with.

***ACTION EXERCISES***

1. Determine your personal preference or dominant style of learning and absorbing information. What is it?
2. Identify the dominant style of your boss and your key staff members. Ask them directly how they like to receive information, and then give it to them in that form.

FOURTEEN

# Systematic Problem Solving Revisited

**THERE ARE** certain qualities of geniuses that have been observed of highly intelligent people throughout the ages. One of these qualities is that they approach each problem in their field systematically and logically.

This powerful method is aimed at keeping emotions out of the problem-solving methodology as long as possible. It forces the problem solver to take a more objective view of the problem and work it through, step-by-step.

There are nine steps to this systematic method of problem solving.

## Assume a Logical Solution

Step one is for you to always assume a logical solution to any problem, difficulty, or goal. Your attitude toward a problem at the beginning is going to determine whether you release your creativity or keep it locked up. Approach every problem or difficulty as though there were a logical, practical solution just waiting to be found.

One of your goals as a creative thinker is to keep calm and unemotional as much as possible throughout the creative thinking process.

## Use Positive Language

Step two, as I described previously, is for you to use positive language to describe the problem or difficulty. Instead of calling something a problem, you should use the word *situation.* Whereas a problem conjures up a negative condition that activates the emotional brain, a situation is neutral and enables you to deal with the difficulty in a calm, objective manner.

Even better is for you to use the word *challenge* rather than problem. A challenge is something that you rise to, that brings out the best in you, whereas a problem is an obstacle or negative condition that causes stress or frustration.

The best word of all is *opportunity.* When you begin to define each situation you face as a challenge or opportunity, you begin to see possibilities that may have been blocked or obscured up till now.

## Define It Clearly

Step three is for you to define the situation clearly, whatever it is. What is the situation, exactly? Accurate diagnosis is half the cure. When discussing a difficult situation with a group, use a whiteboard or flipchart to write out a definition of the situation so clearly that everyone agrees with it.

Often, a problem well defined, especially as a challenge or opportunity, can be quickly solved once it becomes clear to everyone.

## Diagnose the Situation

Step four is to ask, "What are all the possible causes of this situation?" Just as a doctor conducts a complete series of tests to determine how an illness or ailment came about, the business executive has the job of determining what caused the problem in the first place.

In many cases, the causative factor was a unique event that happened only once and that does not require a systemwide change in activities or operations. In some cases, the problem is a systemic problem that requires a total change in the way the business is run in that area.

## Expand the Possibilities

Step five is to ask, "What are all the possible solutions?" There is a direct relationship between the number of possible solutions that you develop for a problem situation and the quality of the solution that you eventually settle upon in the end.

In the systematic, investigative part of the problem-solving process, your job is to develop the greatest number of possible solutions, including doing nothing at all, before you begin moving to the decision-making phase of the process.

## Make a Decision

Step number six is to make a decision. In many cases, if you have followed the first five steps calmly and logically, the ideal decision will emerge logically as well, as cream rises to the top of the milk.

In most cases, any decision is usually better than no decision at all. If you cannot make a decision at the moment because you need further information, set a deadline for when you will make a final decision. Don't let a problem situation hang in the air with no resolution.

## Assign Who Will Be Responsible

Step seven is to assign specific responsibility. Who is going to do what, and by when? Especially, set a measure for the solution so that everyone can be clear about whether the solution has been achieved.

## Set Deadlines and Take Action

Step eight is to set a deadline. A decision without a deadline is simply a circular discussion. Agree with everyone on the timing of the solution and when progress toward the solution can be determined.

Step nine is for you to *take action immediately*. Implement the solution right away. In the final analysis, action is everything. The faster you take action, the faster you get constructive feedback that enables you to change course and take even more effective actions.

The whole purpose of this problem-solving process is to prepare you and the people around you to take positive, constructive action toward achieving specific, desired results. If action is not taken, then the whole exercise of creative thinking becomes merely a process of intellectual amusement.

Every good solution has not only an action plan, but also a monitoring, controlling, and testing plan built into it so that you can determine whether or not the solution was effective.

## What the Top Executives Do

In my work with more than 1,000 large companies worldwide, I have had the opportunity to sit in with several high-level executives, often billionaires and multibillionaires, and observe them when they are required to deal with a large problem or a crisis in their corporations.

Without exception, I have noticed that top leaders go completely calm when dealing with a problem that causes other people around them to become upset and angry.

Keep your mind calm, clear, and objective whenever you are required to deal with a major setback or problem. Follow the steps outlined in this chapter until they become second nature. You will be pleasantly amazed at the quality of the solutions you come up with and the excellence of the decisions that you make.

### *ACTION EXERCISES*

1. What is the biggest business problem or challenge you are dealing with right now? Define it clearly in writing.

2. List seven different things you could do, including doing nothing, to solve this problem or remove this obstacle.

FIFTEEN

# Practice Zero-Based Thinking

**ZERO-BASED** thinking is a creative thinking technique that helps you approach problems and find solutions from a completely different position. It requires that you put every previous decision on trial for its life on a regular basis, especially when you get new information or gain experience that contradicts or challenges the thinking upon which the decision was made in the first place.

Zero-based thinking comes from the financial concept of zero-based budgeting. In zero-based budgeting, instead of looking at how much to increase or decrease a particular expenditure in an upcoming accounting period, you ask the question, "If we were not spending money in this area already, would we get into this area again today, knowing what we now know?"

## Conduct a KWINK Analysis

This question is called a KWINK analysis. "**K**nowing **W**hat **I** **N**ow **K**now, is there anything that I am doing today that, if I had to do it over again, I would not have gotten into it in the first place?"

Draw a line under all your previous thinking and be prepared to challenge every decision you have ever made with this question.

If you ask this KWINK question and your answer is "No, knowing what I now know, I would not get into this situation again," then your next question is, "How do I get out, and how fast?"

Here is what I have discovered. When your answer to the zero-based thinking question comes back with a "no," it usually means that it is too late to save the situation. The only question now is how long are you going to wait, and how much is it going to cost, before you finally bite the bullet and stop doing what you are doing?

## Three Areas for Zero-Based Thinking

There are three major areas where zero-based thinking is applicable throughout your life and career. The first has to do with *relationships*. Is there any person in your business or personal life who you would not get involved with again today, if you had to do it over, knowing what you now know?

Is there any person that you would not hire, promote, assign, or delegate a task to, knowing what you now know about this person?

Fully 85 percent of your unhappiness, stress, and frustration in life, personal and business, will come from your continuing to associate, live with, or work with someone who, knowing what you now know, you wouldn't get involved with in the first place.

The second area where you apply zero-based thinking has to do with every part of your *business*. Is there anything that you are doing in your business that, knowing what you now know, you would not start up again today if you had to do it over?

Is there any product or service that you are offering that you would not bring to the market, knowing what you now know?

Is there any method of marketing, sales, or business development that, knowing what you now know, you would not start using again today, if you had to do it over?

Is there any process, procedure, or method of doing business that, knowing what you now know, you would not implement again today?

The third area where you apply zero-based thinking is with regard to *investments* of money, time, or emotion. Human beings hate to lose money, for any reason. But many of our very best and most carefully considered decisions about investments of money, both in business and in personal life, will turn out to be wrong to one degree or another. Simply ask yourself, "If I had not invested money in this particular product, service, or activity, knowing what I now know, would I invest the money today?"

If your answer is "no," your next question is, "How do I get out of this situation, and how fast?"

Be willing to cut your losses, to admit you made a mistake, you were wrong, and that based on your current information it was not a good investment. Refuse to throw money down a rat hole by refusing to admit that you made a mistake.

Just as people hate to lose money, they hate to lose time as well. You may have invested an enormous amount of time developing a new product or project, learning a new subject or skill, or taking a particular course of study. Now you realize that, knowing what you now know, it was not a good idea. You have lost your time. It is gone forever. Your solution is to stop investing time in a situation or area where it is clear that your original investment has been lost.

Finally, it is quite common for us to invest an enormous amount of emotion, especially in relationships (business and personal) and in courses of action (study or career directions). Nonetheless, if it is clear that we have made a mistake and that all our emotional investment has been of no use, we must be prepared to write it off and walk away.

In order to think creatively and come up with the best new ideas for the future, you have to be willing to clear out the mental blocks that hold you back from creative thinking. Zero-based thinking is one of the very best tools you can use to remain flexible and open and to become a competent and creative thinker in every area of your life.

***ACTION EXERCISES***

1. Identify one relationship in your life, business or personal, that you would not get into again today, and resolve to end it as soon as possible.
2. Identify one activity in your business or personal life that you would not start up again today, if you had it to do over, and resolve to get out of it immediately.

SIXTEEN

# Face Reality

**FORMER GE** chairman and CEO Jack Welch once said that the most important rule in business is the "reality principle." This is the ability to see the world as it really is, rather than the way that you wish it would be. It is the ability to be perfectly honest with yourself in any situation, no matter how much ego you have invested in being right. When Jack Welch would come into a problem-solving meeting, the first question he would ask was, "What's the reality?"

This should be your question as well. What's the reality? Go through every area of your business and personal life and ask that question. "Is there anything that I am doing that I would not get into again today if I had to do it over, knowing what I now know?"

Sooner or later, the reality will catch up with you. It is not something that you can avoid. Times have changed and the situation that you are in is no longer tenable. It is over. Finished. You will have to move on. The only question is, How long will you wait and how high a price will you pay before you admit the reality?

Happily enough, when you finally admit that, knowing what you now know, you wouldn't get into this situation again, and decide to end it, you will have the two reactions that all people experience. First, you will feel a tremendous sense of relief and even exhilaration. You will be happy, because a burden of stress and frustration has been taken off your shoulders and out of your mind. Second, you will ask yourself, "Why didn't I do this a long time ago?"

## No Growth Situation

One of my clients started and built a reasonably successful company. But at a certain point, business leveled off in sales and was not able to grow any further. This lack of growth generated a good deal of frustration and unhappiness for my friend, and for many other people in the company. No matter what they did, they couldn't seem to keep up with or get ahead of their competition.

Of course, they blamed their problems on a variety of factors, such as competition, the current economy, changes in technology, ineffective advertising, product and service problems and defects, and so on.

The transformation in their business came when the president finally realized that it was his best friend, who had been with the company since the beginning, who was the real problem and roadblock to any future success. He had made a valuable contribution when the company was small and growing but was totally overwhelmed by the complexities of running a larger organization.

When my client replaced his friend (which was a stressful and expensive management decision), the logjam in the company was broken. The company brought in new people who were much more competent and capable and who were experienced at sales, marketing, financing, and positioning against competition. Within twelve months, the company's sales and profits had doubled, and they continue to grow to this day.

## Courage Is the Key

It takes tremendous courage for you to stand back and look honestly and objectively at your life and work. You often have to admit that you made a mistake, or that a decision you made earlier has turned out to be the wrong decision, based on the situation as it is today.

Mark McCormack, a billionaire executive who built the biggest sports marketing company in the world, wrote in his book, *What They Don't Teach You at Harvard Business School*, that there were three statements that an effective executive had to learn to use early and often if he wanted to succeed in a fast-changing, turbulent marketplace.

First, you have to learn to say the words, "I was wrong." According to the American Management Association, 70 percent of management decisions will turn out to be wrong in the fullness of time. They will be a little bit wrong, a lot wrong, or complete disasters. As soon as you realize that you have made a mistake of any kind, be prepared to admit that you were wrong and minimize the damage as much as possible.

The second statement you must learn to use early and often is, "I made a mistake."

It's been said that "every large problem was once a small problem and could have been solved easily at that time." It is amazing how many mistakes are allowed to become larger and larger, like a prairie fire, when they could have been solved quickly at an earlier stage by someone having the ego strength to simply admit, "I made a mistake."

## Develop Mental Flexibility

The third statement you must learn to say is, "I changed my mind."

Many people, as a result of childhood experiences, grew up with the idea that it is a sign of weakness to change their minds or to reverse a decision that they have made. But this is not the case. In a time of rapid change, it is a mark of courage, character, and competence to realize that the situation has changed and that you must change your thinking as well if you are going to survive and thrive.

In my company, I continually remind people that it is all right to make a mistake. One new piece of information from the marketplace can completely invalidate the very best thinking that you have done up to this point. You could develop a complete strategic plan on Friday and get a new piece of information on Monday that forces you to throw it away and start over.

#### ***ACTION EXERCISES***

1. Ask yourself, "Am I seeing the situation as it really is, or as I hope it would be?" Be completely honest with yourself. Sooner or later, you will have to face the reality.
2. Become comfortable saying the magic words, "I was wrong. I made a mistake. I changed my mind."

SEVENTEEN

# Don't Let Roadblocks Be a Problem

**ON THE PATH** to achieving any business or personal goal, there will be roadblocks and obstacles. Some will be clear and obvious, and others will be invisible and unexpected. Some obstacles will be what Donald Rumsfeld called "the unknown unknowns."

We discussed the idea of "pressing problems" in earlier chapters. One of the primary uses of creativity is to identify all the factors that are holding you back from achieving your most important goals and objectives. You must then go through these issues to determine your biggest obstacle, the removal of which can help you achieve your goals faster than the removal of any other obstacle.

## The Rock in the Road

Imagine yourself with a group of people, walking along a mountain road. You come around a turn and there before you is a huge rock that has fallen and is now blocking your passage. In this metaphor, the purpose of an organization is to bring together the different talents and skills necessary to remove this "rock in the road" that is stopping you from making any further progress.

A group of my business associates in Los Angeles put together a high-tech company offering a valuable service to publicly traded companies. They continually upgraded the product, and the customers who used it reported excellent results. The problem was that they did not have enough business to break even, much less to make a profit. They were continually raising new funds from prospective investors just to stay alive. This situation continued for several years.

Then they had a great revelation, one that is not uncommon to start-ups in high-tech industries. They realized that their problem was not the need to continually improve their technology but to sell their technology to more customers. Because they came from technical backgrounds, it had never occurred to them that the product or service is secondary to the ability to sell it in sufficient quantities to make a profit.

## Focus on Sales

With this revelation, they turned their attention to finding an outstanding sales professional, someone who is called an "outperformer," who could drive the sales of their product to a larger market. Once they were clear about the solution they needed, they very soon found the right person with the right set of sales skills.

Within one year, with the sales executive working aggressively fifty hours a week, the company went from losses to profits. In the second year, profits doubled and then tripled. In the third year, profits went up ten times over anything that the company had ever imagined in the past. The stock price jumped ten times as well, and all the financial problems that had accumulated over the years were quickly resolved.

What is your "rock"? What is the number one obstacle that is holding you back from achieving the personal or financial results you desire? Whatever it is, you must be absolutely clear about your biggest problem, and then you must somehow get around, over, or through this major rock in order to achieve your most important goal.

Identifying your major rock and focusing all your mental energies on blasting that obstacle out of the way will help you to make more progress in a short time than if you were to remove all the other small obstacles in your way.

## The Cluster Problem

In business, the obstacle or obstacles that are holding you back often appear as a complicated or "cluster problem." This is a problem that has many little factors, all of which are conspiring together to hold you back from making the kind of progress you want.

However, within a complex, cluster-like problem, there always seems to be one major problem that must be solved before all the minor problems can be solved. Once the major problem is resolved or removed, all the smaller problems seem to take care of themselves quite quickly.

The biggest mistake that people make is that they prefer to do what is fun and easy rather than what is right, necessary, and difficult. They like to toy around with all the little obstacles and day-to-day problems. They distract themselves and ignore the massive rock or limiting factor that is the primary obstacle holding them back.

***ACTION EXERCISES***

1. Identify the biggest single obstacle, inside or outside your business, that is limiting your sales and profitability today.
2. Become comfortable saying these magic words: "I was wrong. I made a mistake. I changed my mind."

EIGHTEEN

# The Seven Sources of Innovation

**IN PETER DRUCKER'S** excellent book *Innovation and Entrepreneurship,* he describes the seven major sources of innovation for businesses of all kinds. As you look for creative ways to grow your business, start with these seven sources of innovation.

## The Unexpected Event

The unexpected event—the unexpected success, failure, or outside event that leads to or indicates a new business opportunity—is often the breakthrough innovation that changes an entire industry.

Pierre Omidyar had a collection of Pez candy dispensers that he wanted to sell in the open market. Because there was no website available for him, he created eBay to sell them to the highest bidder. The response was so immediate and enormous that he decided to offer additional products for sale using the eBay auction model. This unexpected success, which he recognized and capitalized on quickly, made him one of the richest men in the world.

Many innovative breakthroughs in business are triggered by an unexpected failure as well. Often, an unexpected product failure leads to a rethinking and redesign that drives the creation of a product that becomes hugely popular.

## Incongruity

Another source of innovation is an incongruity between the reality of what is and what "ought" to be. In other words, an incongruity develops when things are supposed to happen in a certain way and they don't.

Look around your business today. Is there anything that is happening in your business, and in market demand, that is different from what you had originally expected? These incongruities could all be sources of innovative products and services that could transform your business.

## Process Need

Another major source of innovation is process need. There is a breakthrough in technology, a technique, or a system that you need inside the company to overcome a problem or a shortcoming, which often requires the development of a process with commercial applications. It may be something you can use to overcome a limiting factor that is holding you back from market dominance.

When Tom Monaghan came up with the idea of delivering pizza in thirty minutes or less, the owners of the pizza restaurant where he worked told him that it simply could not be done. Each pizza had to be prepared to order before being baked, boxed, and sent out to the person who ordered it. The process could not be done in less than thirty minutes.

Monaghan's breakthrough was simple. Based on his experience delivering pizzas and some market research, he found that 20 percent of the pizzas offered accounted for 80 percent of the pizzas ordered. He then decided to open his own pizza restaurant and produce only eight pizzas—the most popular in terms of size and ingredients. He pre-prepared the most popular pizzas and had them ready for baking when the orders came in. Before the dust had settled, Domino's Pizza had 8,000 restaurants worldwide.

How could you change or develop a process that would allow you to serve your customers better, faster, cheaper, or more conveniently than your competitors? One small change or improvement in the process of producing or delivering your product can give you the "winning edge" in your industry.

## Changes in Industry Structure

Changes in industry structure, as a result of a variety of different causes, are a fourth source of innovation. A good example is the introduction of the Apple iPhone in 2006, which spurred Samsung into the market with its Android-based smartphones. Within five years, both BlackBerry, which dominated the world of business phones, and Nokia, which dominated the world of cell phones, were down to less than 10 percent of their previous market shares.

Every new discovery, every new breakthrough in technology, every competitive initiative that changes or disrupts an industry, opens up opportunities for new products and services that can be hugely profitable in today's fast-changing markets.

## Demographic Changes

Demographic changes are generating major innovations in the public and private sectors of our country and worldwide. Over the next twenty years, baby boomers are going to be retiring at a rate of 10,000 per day. The needs, wants, and desires of senior citizens—in lifestyle, health, medicine, travel, transportation, and every other field—are creating huge markets for new products and services and making fortunes for many innovative executives and companies.

The shift in population in the U.S. toward the warmer states of the south and the west, away from the north and the East Coast, has created tremendous changes and opportunities in home construction, retail, medical care, lifestyle products and services, Medicare, and countless other areas.

One of the most profound changes is the population movement away from high-tax, high-regulation states to low-tax, low-regulation states. Texas alone, with no income tax and a business-favorable regulatory system, has created more new jobs in the last five years than all the other forty-nine states put together. These trends will continue.

## Changes in Values and Perceptions

Changes in perceptions can also lead to innovation. For example, there is a much greater emphasis on health foods and fitness today than there was in the last generation. This concern for longer life, better health, and more energy has fueled the organic food craze and the vitamin industry. The average life span has increased from 60 years of age in 1935 to 80 years in 2014. More people want to live longer, better, and healthier lives than ever before. This desire on the part of millions of relatively affluent consumers is creating unlimited business opportunities for innovative entrepreneurs who can develop new products and services to satisfy these needs.

## New Knowledge

New knowledge, both scientific and nonscientific, creates new economic trends, opportunities, and even completely new industries.

The ability to put most of the functions of a personal computer on a tablet device such as the Apple iPad has transformed the world of mobile computing, leading to ever-declining sales of PCs and price wars that are decimating many of the leading companies in the personal computer industry. At the same time, many millions and billions of dollars of sales and revenue are being created by those companies creating new mobile applications and services for tablet owners.

At the same time, new knowledge is the least dependable source of innovation because it takes so long to get into the marketplace, and it is very difficult to know exactly what will happen as a result of this new knowledge.

### *ACTION EXERCISES*

1. Imagine that you were starting your business over again today, with your current knowledge and experience and with the world changing rapidly around you. What would you start up, and what would you discontinue?
2. Identify the most important trends in your business world today and project forward five years to determine the products and services you will have to be offering to survive and thrive at that time.

NINETEEN

# Ten Creative Solutions to Obsolete Products

**WHATEVER PRODUCTS** or services have allowed you to reach the place you are in your business or industry today, they are not enough to get you very much further. Fully 80 percent of the products and services that people will be using in five years do not exist today. This means that, on average, 20 percent of products and services offered in the market today, including yours, will be obsolete within twelve months and will need to be replaced with products and services that are more attractive to more customers.

While at first glance the problem of obsolescence may seem daunting, once again creative solutions will be sparked by the right questions. Continually ask questions about your products or services to stimulate ideas to make them more marketable or profitable.

Here are some questions that you can ask and answer on a regular basis.

1. *Could you put your products or services to other uses?* Could they be used by other companies, other industries, or other customers?

One of our rules is that if you have a good product or service and your customers are not buying it, you should change your customers rather than change your product. Perhaps you are aiming your marketing and sales efforts at the wrong target.

2. *Could you adapt, copy, or emulate what someone else is doing to make your products or services better?* One of the smartest things that you can do in business is to admire your successful competitors and then look for ways to do them one better.

You can look for ways to transfer an innovation or a technology from one industry to another. Henry Ford got the idea for the production line by watching a meatpacking plant in operation.

What examples of successful businesses around you could be copied to make your business operate more efficiently and profitably?

3. *Could you modify, change, or repackage your existing product so that it performs or looks like something different?* Could you put a new twist on it? Walt Disney and Roy Disney were visiting Tivoli Gardens in Copenhagen in the late 1940s and noticed that the park was spotless, with not so much as

a matchstick or piece of paper anywhere. By contrast, almost all amusement parks in America, large and small, including county fairs and rodeos, were dirty and littered with trash, with food thrown on the ground. At that moment, Walt conceived of Disneyland. He said, "I'm going to build an amusement park that is so clean and beautiful that parents will bring their children from everywhere to visit it over and over again." The rest is history.

**4.** *Could you magnify the product?* Could you make it bigger, stronger, or shinier? Could you increase it in some way in order to make it more attractive?

We take our whole family each year for a one-week Caribbean cruise on the Allure of the Seas cruise liner. When it was built, it was the largest cruise ship in history, holding 5,000 people. It includes seven completely different environments, from subtropical to desert, and has many European and American boardwalk-style restaurants.

**5.** *Could you minimize it?* Could you make it smaller, shorter, or more economic in scale? What could you remove or subtract from it to make it simpler? Could you break it down into its component parts to sell separately?

**6.** *How about a substitute?* Could you use a different material or process or manufacturing or distribution method, or use a different way of advertising or packaging?

**7.** *Could you rearrange or interchange components in your product or service?* In doing so, is there some way to make your product or service more attractive, more salable, cheaper, or more desirable to more customers?

**8.** *Could you reverse your thinking and take a completely opposite approach to what you're currently doing?* One of the reversals that I used many years ago was instead of lowering the price to clear out a serious product overstock, I raised the price. Because of the higher perceived value, and a couple of special bonuses that we included, we cleared out a product that we had not been able to move for several months.

**9.** *Could you combine your product with something else?* Could you bundle it with other items to make a higher-value offering?

By bundling everything that the customer needs in a particular product or service into a single offering at a single price, you dramatically decrease the complexities and uncertainties of buying and simultaneously increase the attractiveness of your product or service.

**10.** *Can you find value in a by-product?* Sometimes you can. There is the story about a manufacturer of adhesive ECG electrodes. These electrodes were three-inch circles with a three-quarter-inch hole punched out of the center and discarded.

One day the manufacturer decided to package the waste product or "dots." They found dozens of uses—as bumpers to stop doors and drawers from slamming, or to keep pictures from scraping the walls, or to help identify passengers' luggage at the airport. The manufacturer gave away these "dots" to its customers, who were delighted, and it cost the company virtually nothing.

Think and see the world through the minds and eyes of your customers. What do your customers want and need that they are willing to pay for? How could you provide your customers with a buying experience that is superior to that of your competitors? There is no end to answers to these questions.

***ACTION EXERCISES***

1. Identify three specific ways that you could improve your current product or service offerings to make them more attractive to your customers.

2. Phone ten of your best customers and ask them for their opinions and advice on how you could make your products or services more attractive and useful to them. You will probably be astonished at the number of good ideas they will give you.

TWENTY

# The Value-Engineering Principle

**VALUE ENGINEERING** is a simple method of evaluating the usefulness of a new product by asking some key questions:

1. What is the product or service? Describe it through the mind of the consumer.
2. What does it do? Exactly? How does it improve the life or work of the customer?
3. What does it cost?
4. What else will do the same job?
5. What does that alternative cost?

Human beings are often described as "homo economicus," or economic man (or woman). We always seek to get the very most at the lowest possible cost, all things considered. If you have a product or a service that is similar to that of others in the hearts and minds of your customers, your price has to be equivalent to or lower than your competitors if you want to survive and thrive in any market.

Very often, this value-engineering principle will lead you to outsourcing. You may find that instead of doing something in-house, you could find another company with better capacities or facilities and save money by having this outside company do the job.

This need to offer the very best products and services at the very lowest price possible is the driving force behind outsourcing and offshoring. People's desire for low prices is what drives world manufacturing from countries with high production and high labor costs to countries in Asia and Africa with lower costs of labor and production.

***ACTION EXERCISES***

1. Describe your products or services in terms of what they do to improve the life or work of your customer. How else could you bring about this improvement, or another improvement, for your customers?

2. People buy a product or service to do a job for them that they want and need to be done. What additional jobs do your customers need done that you can offer or develop products or services to accomplish?

TWENTY-ONE

# Evaluate Your Ideas

**IDEAS ARE** a dime a dozen. Eighty percent of new products produced, even after extensive research and testing, will fail, and 99 percent of new ideas turn out to be impractical. Before falling in love with your ideas, subject them to rigorous evaluation.

First of all, is it effective? Will it work? Will it make a meaningful difference? Is it a good enough idea to make a meaningful improvement over the current situation?

## Efficiency

Is your new product or service efficient? Is it a significant improvement over the status quo? I have seen many people come into the market with their goods and services thinking people will buy them because they are going to sell them with great skill and determination. What you need to ask, though, is this: "Why would customers stop buying something they are already happy with and buy your product instead?"

Your product always has to be a significant improvement over what currently exists.

## Compatibility

Is your new product or service compatible with human nature? Is it compatible with the way people like to shop? Today, people are shopping online for the things that they want rather than going through the hassle and inconvenience of getting in their cars and driving across town to buy from a store. Many other people will still travel to the store for the buying experience. This is because people like to touch, taste, smell, and feel things before they buy them. They like the experience of live shopping.

Which of these methods of buying is most popular with the products you sell?

## Do You Like It?

Do you like the new product or service innovation yourself? Would you buy it and use it in your home or business? Would you recommend it or sell it to your mother, father, brother, sister, or best friend? The most successful innovative breakthroughs in the fastest-growing companies are those that the company owners and executives really believe in, enjoy using, and would recommend to anybody.

Is your new product or service idea compatible with your goals? Is it an idea to which you or someone else can make a total commitment? If it is not compatible with what you want to accomplish in your life so that you can commit yourself wholeheartedly, maybe you should pass it on to someone else.

## Is It Simple?

Finally, is it simple? In the final analysis, almost all great innovations are simple. They can be explained in twenty-five words or less. The customer in the marketplace can hear a description of the innovation and say, "Yes, that's good. That's what I want. I'll take it. That's what I need."

Simplicity is the key to success in introducing a new product or service because it has to be sold by ordinary people, and ordinary people are not necessarily experts in all the offerings they sell. It has to be bought by ordinary people, and ordinary people cannot be expected to understand the intricacies of the product or service. They might not easily comprehend the product or its true value.

Is the timing right? Is it practical now? Sometimes an idea comes to market too soon or too late. A great idea for a luxury product is likely to have trouble catching on in a recession. Similarly, a discount item may flop in a boom time.

Is it feasible? Is it worth it to engage in the time, work, and cost to produce and deliver the new product or service?

***ACTION EXERCISES***

1. Discipline yourself to ask the "brutal questions" about your product or service idea, and especially solicit the opinions of your current and potential customers before you invest in bringing a new product or service to the market.

2. Remember the Golden Rules of business success. Rule number one: The customer is always right. Rule number two: When in doubt, refer back to rule number one.

# Conclusion

**YOU ARE** a potential genius. You have more potential than you could use in a hundred lifetimes. According to Tony Buzan, the brain expert, the number of thoughts and ideas that you generate using your 100-billion-cell brain is greater than all the molecules in all the known universe.

You have within you, right now, the ability to develop a continuous stream of great ideas to produce, market, and sell more and better products and services to more people in more markets than you ever have before. By asking and answering the questions posed in this book, your mind will continually dance with new ideas, sparkling like a Christmas tree with insights, every single day.

# INDEX